Places in American History

The Alamo

by Frances E. Ruffin

Reading consultant: Susan Nations, M.Ed., author/literacy coach/consultant in literacy development

WEEKLY WR READER®
EARLY LEARNING LIBRARY

Please visit our web site at: www.earlyliteracy.cc
For a free color catalog describing Weekly Reader® Early Learning Library's
list of high-quality books, call 1-877-445-5824 (USA) or 1-800-387-3178 (Canada).
Weekly Reader® Early Learning Library's fax: (414) 336-0164.

Library of Congress Cataloging-in-Publication Data

Ruffin, Frances E.
    The Alamo / by Frances E. Ruffin.
        p. cm. — (Places in American history)
    Includes bibliographical references and index.
    ISBN 0-8368-6407-7 (lib. bdg.)
    ISBN 0-8368-6414-X (softcover)
    1. Alamo (San Antonio, Tex.)—Juvenile literature. 2. Alamo (San Antonio, Tex.)—Siege, 1836—Juvenile
literature. 3. Texas—History—To 1846—Juvenile literature. 4. San Antonio (Tex.)—Buildings, structures,
etc.—Juvenile literature. I. Title.
    F390.R84   2006
    976.4'03—dc22
                                                                        2005026268

This edition first published in 2006 by
Weekly Reader® Early Learning Library
A Member of the WRC Media Family of Companies
330 West Olive Street, Suite 100
Milwaukee, WI 53212 USA

Copyright © 2006 by Weekly Reader® Early Learning Library

Managing Editor: Valerie J. Weber
Editor: Barbara Kiely Miller
Art direction: Tammy West
Graphic design: Dave Kowalski
Photo research: Diane Laska-Swanke

Photo credits: Cover, title, pp. 4, 18 © James P. Rowan; p. 5 Dave Kowalski/© Weekly Reader Early
Learning Library, 2006; pp. 6, 7 © Kean Collection/Getty Images; pp. 8, 9, 11, 13 © North Wind Picture
Archives; p. 10 © Hulton Archive/Getty Images; p. 12 Stefan Chabluk and Dave Kowalski/© Weekly
Reader Early Learning Library, 2006; pp. 15, 16 © Library of Congress; p. 17 © Joe Raedle/Getty Images;
pp. 19, 20 © A. Y. Owen/Time & Life Pictures/Getty Images

Printed in the United States of America

1 2 3 4 5 6 7 8 9 10 09 08 07 06

Table of Contents

The Alamo was one of five missions that the Spanish built along the San Antonio River.

A Fort That Means Freedom

The Alamo is the most famous place in Texas. It is a church that was once part of a fort. Here, a small group of Texans fought against a large Mexican army. They fought to free Texas from Mexico. The Alamo stands for their courage.

The Alamo is almost three hundred years old. It was built near the San Antonio River. A small town stood on the other side of the river. That town is now the city of San Antonio, Texas.

The state of Texas used to be part of Mexico.

UNITED STATES TERRITORY

TEXAS

MEXICO

Austin

San Antonio Houston

San Antonio River

Rio Grande

United States and U.S. territory
Mexico and Mexican territory
Present-day state boundaries

Gulf
of
Mexico

The mission's priests used to lived in the barracks (*left*). Later, Mexican and Texan soldiers lived there.

The Alamo Mission

Spain once owned Texas and Mexico. The Spanish built missions in Texas. In missions, priests teach other people about their beliefs. A church and a school stood at the mission. Native Americans lived nearby. Their children went to its school.

A wall was built around the mission to protect it. Later, other buildings were added. In 1793, the mission closed. Ten years later, Spanish soldiers moved to the mission. They renamed it the "Alamo." This word is Spanish for cottonwood, a type of tree.

The wall around the mission was built of stone and clay.

A Battle for Texas

In 1821, Mexico won its freedom from Spain. Texas was now a state of Mexico. Many people from the United States moved to Texas. Stephen Austin brought three hundred families to live there in 1821. Thousands of people came later. The people from the United States were called Anglos. Some settled in the town near the Alamo.

Stephen Austin worked for the rights of the Anglos in Texas.

The Mexican government said there were too many Anglo settlers. Mexico passed a law to stop new Anglos from moving to Texas. The Anglos thought this and other Mexican laws were unfair. They wanted their rights and would fight for them. They were called rebels. The leader of Mexico, Antonio López de Santa Anna wanted to destroy the rebels.

Antonio López de Santa Anna was the president of Mexico and the leader of its army.

Sam Houston led the rebel army. A small group of Texans took over the Alamo. They asked people in the United States for help. James Bowie bought and sold land and slaves. He came with thirty men. A famous hunter from Tennessee, Davy Crockett, came with a dozen men. Army officer William Travis brought thirty men. He was put in charge of the fort.

Before coming to Texas, Davy Crockett was a law maker in the U.S. government. He also fought in a war against Creek Indians.

After marching to the Alamo, the Mexican army
waited almost two weeks before attacking the fort.

On February 23, 1836, Santa Anna arrived outside
of San Antonio. He brought an army of four
thousand men. Texan soldiers headed toward the
fort. Anglo and Mexican familes fled to the Alamo.
They all wanted to be safe behind its walls.

The Mexican army stayed outside the Alamo for thirteen days. Less than two hundred men were inside the Alamo. They fired canons and rifles at the Mexican army. The Mexicans fired canons in return. Before sunrise on March 6, Santa Anna's men surrounded the fort. They climbed the walls of the Alamo and attacked the men inside.

This diagram shows the Alamo at the time of the 1836 battle. The Texans built high platforms for their canons.

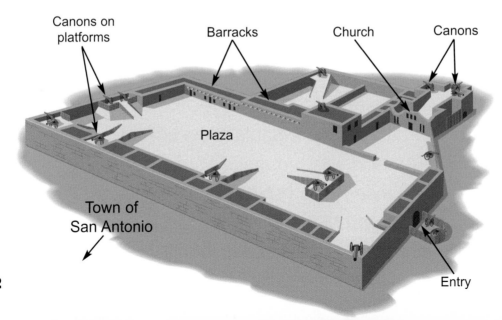

Canons on platforms

Barracks

Church

Canons

Plaza

Town of San Antonio

Entry

All of the men defending the Alamo were killed. Hundreds of Mexican soldiers were also killed or hurt. Women and children hiding in the church were safe. The battle badly damaged the Alamo's buildings. Mexican soldiers knocked down the fort's walls.

© North Wind Picture Archives

After a fierce and deadly fight, the Mexican army captured the Alamo fort.

Remembering the Alamo

Texans did not forget the brave men who died at the Alamo. Texans fought another battle to become free from Mexico. They shouted, "Remember the Alamo" to help them win. Texas became independent, or free, from Mexico. In December 1845, Texas joined the United States. Cities in Texas were named for leaders Stephen Austin and Sam Houston.

Texas has flown the same flag as both an independent nation, the Republic of Texas, and a U.S. state.

The United States Army used the Alamo for many years. Other groups used the Alamo as well. They knocked down many buildings. Their new buildings covered up parts of the mission.

New buildings covered areas where parts of the Alamo once stood.

Land along Alamo Plaza was bought and added to the Alamo grounds.

Texans, however, wanted to honor the people who fought at the Alamo. By 1905, the State of Texas owned the Alamo. It asked a group of Texan women to take care of the Alamo. The group raised money to make the grounds around the Alamo bigger.

Visiting the Alamo

Today, more than three million people visit the Alamo each year. The Alamo's mission church still stands. The long barracks where the mission's priests and soldiers lived also remain. The barracks are now a museum.

People in costume act out the fall of the Alamo.

This artwork hangs at the Alamo. It shows men who helped the Texans marching toward the fort.

A large model of the famous 1836 battle stands in the Alamo museum. It shows figures of people who fought at the Alamo.

Visitors can also find a ring. The Alamo's leader, William Travis, gave the ring to a young girl during the battle. The little girl had hidden in the church during the fighting. William Travis died in battle.

Visitors can also see Jim Bowie's knife and Davy Crockett's vest. They can see rifles and canons used in the battle.

Visitors to the Alamo can see the rifle found next to Davy Crockett's body. Crockett was one of the last men standing after the Mexican army captured the Alamo.

A large monument outside honors the men who died guarding the Alamo. Their names are carved in the monument. The Alamo helps people remember these brave men. It reminds everyone of their fight for freedom.

This large monument at the Alamo helps visitors remember the men who died as heroes.

Alamo Time Line

1718	The Spanish build the Misión San Antonio de Valero.
1724	The mission church and school are rebuilt at their current location.
1821	Many Anglo settlers move to Texas.
1836	The Alamo falls to the Mexican army.
1845	Texas becomes the twenty-eighth state of the United States of America.
1850	The U.S. Army rebuilds parts of the Alamo.
1905	The State of Texas buys the Alamo. Texas gives the Alamo to a group called the Daughters of the Republic of Texas to take care of.

Glossary

Anglos — white, English-speaking people who are not Hispanic

barracks — buildings used to house soldiers or workers

courage — the inner strength that lets a person bravely face danger, fear, or difficulty

fort — an area or building made stronger to protect against attacks. Walls usually surround forts.

mission — a building where people try to teach others about their religion

monument — a building or statue made in memory of a person or event

rebel — a person who refuses to obey or fights against the government or someone in charge

slaves — people who are owned by other people and made to work without pay. They are not free.

For More Information

Books

The Alamo. Pull Ahead Books (series). Kristin L. Nelson (Lerner Pubishing)

The Alamo. Symbols of Freedom (series). Ted Schaefer (Heinemann)

Davy Crockett. Photo-Illustrated Biographies (series). Kathy Feeney (Bridgestone Books)

Life at the Alamo. Picture the Past (series). Sally Senzell Isaacs (Heinemann Library)

Web Sites

The Alamo

www.enchantedlearning.com/history/us/monuments/alamo/index.shtml

Read more about the Alamo, Texas, and Davy Crockett.

The Alamo: Just for Kids

www.thealamo.org/just_for_kids.html

Play games and work on puzzles about the Alamo's symbols and heros.

Index

About the Author

Frances E. Ruffin has written more than twenty-four books for children. She enjoys reading and writing about the lives of famous and ordinary people. She lives in New York City with her son, Timothy, a young writer who is writing his first novel.